Harry Truman

A biography of Harry Truman, an American President

Table of Contents

Introduction

Thank you for taking the time to pick up this book about Harry S. Truman, the 33rd President of the United States of America.

This book aims to serve as a biography of Harry S. Truman, and explores the incredible life that he lived.

In the following chapters you will learn stories of Harry's childhood, his career in the Army, his family life, and his unlikely journey to presidency.

You will also discover how much positive change that Harry S. Truman was responsible for during his time in office, as well as how forward thinking and revolutionary he was for the time.

At the completion of this book you should have a great understanding of Harry Truman and what type of a President and man he truly was.

Once again, thanks for choosing this book, I hope you find it to be enjoyable.

Chapter 1: Harry's Formative Years

Harry S. Truman, the man without a middle name. The middle initial, "S", really did not stand for anything. Harry's grandfathers argued over who he should be named after. Anderson Truman felt he should have his middle name which was Shipp, and Solomon Young thought he should have his first name, Solomon. So, Harry's parents in the end finally just decided that "S" would be his middle initial and be done with the squabbling.

Harry was born in Lamar, Missouri. Harry's grandparents came from Shelby County, Kentucky to Missouri. They passed down a legacy that is rarely seen today. A legacy of independence, hard work and integrity. Harry's family was of German, French, Scots-Irish, and English origin. Harry grew up being surrounded by strong-willed but loving and doting parents, grandparents, and all kinds of relatives. It was these kind of bonds that would allow Harry to accept himself as the person he was and face whatever external problems he might have. Lamar was a small town that was a couple of hours from Springfield, Missouri or a couple of hours from Kansas City, Missouri. He was born on May 8, 1884, to parents Martha and John Truman. Harry had a brother, named John Vivian (1886-1965) and a sister, whose name was Mary Jane (1889-1978).

Harry suffered from diphtheria at ten years old and was paralyzed in his legs, arms, and throat for six months. He had become so weak and so thin that he had to pushed around in a baby carriage. There was no diphtheria antitoxin available at that time, so they treated him with ipecac and whiskey. When Harry got older, he hated the "medicines" he had been given as a child.

Harry was also diagnosed with an eye problem that was considered "rare" in that day. It was called "flat eyeballs." He had to wear glasses that were very thick when he turned eight years old. Harry's mother had been teaching him to read from the family Bible and had noticed that while he could see large print in the Bible, he struggled to see cars coming down the road or read newsprint. When 4th of July came along and they were celebrating in Grandview, Harry would jump at all the exploding sounds but was not able to see the beautiful showers of fireworks. Today this is called near-sightedness. What makes this issue more than interesting is one possible cause for near-sightedness in children is diphtheria. It can paralyze the ciliary muscle, the muscle that allows the eye to focus. There are some historians who argue as to that being the real reason as to why Harry had problems with his eyes.

In 1890, it was decided the family would move to Independence, Missouri which was only ten miles from Kansas City, Missouri. While living in Independence, Harry worked for their Jewish neighbors as the Shabbos goy for, doing work for them on Shabbos because their religion would not let them work during this time.

Harry suffered his fair share of childhood accidents. The poor lad nearly choked to death on a peach pit that had lodged in his throat, but his mother saved his life by pushing the peach pit on down his throat with her finger.

Vivian, Harry's younger brother, had long, curly hair and his mother simply would not cut it. The curls drove Harry's Grandpa Young crazy, and he took it upon himself to take care of Vivian's long hair. One day, he had Harry help him, and they carried the highchair out to the porch, and Grandpa Young cut off Vivian's beautiful curls. Harry's mother was livid! Having watched all of this, Harry a few days later decided he would do something with his hair. He got the highchair, pulled it up to the mirror so he could look at the back of his head and because he leaned over so much, he fell over backward and broke his collar bone.

One day Harry was playing outside and happened to slam the cellar door shut – on his foot no less and it cut off the end of his big toe. Here comes Harry's mother again to the rescue who held the end of the toe in place till Dr. Tom could get to their house. The family doctor reattached it, used a coating of iodoform, wrapped the toe up, and the toe stayed in place and grew back on where it should!

As children living on the farm, Harry, Vivian and their sister had some pets. Harry liked riding the black Shetland pony his father had given to him, and he rode him all over the farm. They had a black and tan dog they named Tandy and a Maltese bobtailed cat named Bob. The cat got his name because one day while he was sleeping in front of the fireplace a hot coal popped out on the end of his tail and burned off about an inch of it.

Many of the residents in Independence had moved from the Upper South states, bringing southern culture and social traditions with them. The black occupants lived over in the segregated portion of the town.

There were several in Truman's family that had once owned slaves, or they at least still held their pro-slavery views. Some supported openly the Confederacy, and Truman was raised during a time that still entertained racist views. When Harry started his political career, others tried to get him to join the KKK – Ku Klux Klan, but he declined.

Harry had a lot of trouble in his younger days. It was a real effort for him to make friends and he always felt uncomfortable in the presence of girls.

When Harry was fourteen-years-old, he worked at J.H. Clinton's Drug Store in Independence, Missouri. He worked seven days a week. He would go in at seven in the morning until time for school and then from four after school until ten at night; then all day on Saturday and Sunday. His job was wiping off bottles, mopping the floors, making ice cream, and waiting on customers. His first pay day was three silver dollars. In that day and at that time it looked like three million. He bought a present for his mother and tried to give the rest to his father, but his dad would not take it from Harry; he had earned it.

Harry turned to reading and music instead of girls. He loved the piano and for a while pursued being a concert pianist. Harry was serious when it came to the piano. He practiced with self-discipline, on the upright Kimball the family owned. His music teacher arranged for him to meet Ignace Paderewski, a famous concert pianist. He was thrilled with the opportunity. In his spare time, Harry worked as an usher at a Kansas City theater to get free access to shows and performances. "The Girl from Utah" was one musical that for some reason seemed to have special meaning to Harry.

Harry also had a love for books. They took him places he would never go. They were windows to the world. That early passion for learning was instilled in him by his mother and his teachers. It is said that Harry read all 3,000 books in the Independence, Missouri Library, even the encyclopedias, before the age of fifteen. Most kids in that era did not go to school past the seventh grade, but Harry went on to graduate from high school in 1901.

Harry was 17 when he graduated from High School and could not find a job as quickly as he would have liked. His dad lost everything when he speculated on wheat futures.

There was however, one dream that Harry could not get out of his mind, and that was his dream to be a soldier. He wanted badly to attend West Point. But, due to his terrible eyesight, this was not to be a dream to come true.

Harry also briefly worked as a 'page' during the 1900 Democratic National Convention at the Kansas City Convention Hall. There Harry got his first real taste of politics.

The family's financial problems prevented Harry from going to a four-year college. So, Harry decided he would go to a business college close by in Kansas City. The family's financial straits were so desperate at that point; he had to drop out of the business school in order to help the family on the farm. He started working in the mailroom at the Kansas City Star Bank during the summer of 1902. In 1902, Harry made good use of what business college training he had to gain employment as a timekeeper for the Atchison, Topeka & Santa Fe Railway. He slept in hobo camps at night near the rail lines.

In 1903 Harry landed a job at the National Bank of Commerce in Kansas City.

In 1905, Truman found himself working at the Union National Bank for more pay. But in 1906 he left his job at the bank and went back home to work on the family farm located in Grandview, Missouri with his father and his brother. He spent most of the next ten years tending the soil and seeing little profit. He kept the farm's books and shared the burden of the manual labor. Farming was just not his calling.

In 1905, Truman found himself joining the National Guard. This was as close as he could get to military service and he enjoyed the chance to get away from that farm.

Harry noticed Bess for the first time in Sunday School when she was five, and he was six. They were school classmates. But it wasn't until 1910; Harry started dating/courting Bess Wallace. His courting was in earnest and is documented well by one of the best collections of love letters you will probably ever see. He had graduated high school with her but had been so shy with girls at that time he probably never asked her on a date. In 1911, he proposed to her and she politely refused, the reason unknown, but it did not matter, they kept on dating.

Bess came from a well-to-do Independence family. They were third generation owners of a flour mill. Bess excelled in sports and school. She was popular, and she was also privileged. She dressed in the latest styles. At age 18 when her father committed suicide; Bess and her mother went away for 12 months. When they came back to town, they came back to Bess's grandfather's house in Independence, not to their home.

Being on the farm made it tougher to date Bess Wallace. She didn't want anything to do with a farmer. She lived 10 miles away and just to visit her; Harry had to get on a train and then a streetcar. In 1913 Harry bought a used Stafford touring car that was two years old.

In 1913 Harry again asked Bess to marry him. She told him if she ever married anyone, it would be Harry. Secretly, they became engaged.

On November 2, 1914, John Truman, Harry's father died. His father had been injured severely while trying to move a boulder. X-rays revealed a tumor that was blocking his intestines. There was surgery, but there was little hope. Harry had to watch as his father grew weaker every day. John Truman told his son that he was dying a failure. When his father died, it caused Harry much heartache. In others ways, it relieved Harry in the fact that it gave him a better chance to get away from the farm. It just was not in Harry to till the soil. He was just not a farmer.

Harry was brought up in Baptist and Presbyterian Churches; he avoided the revivals and sometimes he would ridicule revival preachers. Harry rarely spoke about religion. Religion to Harry meant ethical behavior along traditional Protestant lines. Most of his war time buddies were Catholics. He got along with soldiers of other Christian denominations as well as the unit's Jewish members. So, just being around Harry, one would think that Harry did not have much to do with religion.

But Harry was more of a Christian than most people realized. The fact that Harry's peers did not know this about his private beliefs is not surprising because, there are just some aspects of a president's private life that are not discussed – religion and marriage. Harry had been brought up knowing the scriptures, and he had said on occasion that 'every problem in the world would be solved if only men would follow the Beatitudes." Harry's favorite verse in Psalms was: "By the rivers of Babylon, there we sat down, yea, we wept, when we remembered Zion." Harry's beloved Bess was Episcopalian, but he felt so strongly about his Baptist upbringing that he remained Baptist; being convinced that it was the religion that the common man could use to be the shortest route to God. Truman was always quoting his grandpa's warning. "If you hear somebody praying too loud, you better run and lock up your smokehouse."

After his father's death, Harry tried two risky adventures and was hoping for a big payoff, but both fell pitifully short. One was a zinc mine in Oklahoma and the other an oil drilling scheme. He wound up in more debt than before.

Years after his father's death, when Harry was asked if his father was a failure, Harry had answered with, "how could he be a failure if his son became President of the United States."

Chapter 2: Harry's Dream of Becoming a Soldier

Come 1917, the United States was about to enter World War I, and Harry decided to rejoin his National Guard unit. If Harry had not memorized the eye chart, he would have never been accepted in the National Guard! The Unit became federalized, and overnight Harry Truman was a part of the 129th Artillery Regiment despite his blindness. He was needed. Bess Wallace told Harry that she did want to get married now, as she cried. Harry asked her to wait till he got back. He didn't think now was a good idea. Harry didn't feel it would be the right thing for her to tie herself down to a perspective cripple.

Being a soldier suited Harry. He rose to Captain and commanded the regiment's successful canteen. He turned his unit; which did not have the best reputation- into a highly-regarded troop.

It was March 1918, and Harry's unit shipped over to France. In July 1918, the officers and Harry's men of the 129th Field Artillery moved to Camp Coetquidan in Brittany, so they could receive advanced training on the use of the new 75 mm field gun while under simulated conditions. This is the point where Harry truly took charge of Battery D. Despite some earlier attempts of his men to try and intimidate him, Harry made them accountable for discipline, and he promised he would be there to back them up. Battery D realized then that Harry knew what he was doing and followed him as a loyal crew for the rest of the war. Harry and his men saw action in the Vosges Mountains to the Argonnes forest. Harry's men guided their equipment and horses over one hundred miles of muddy, crowded back roads to get to the new American section. The march and the five days of intense combat that followed were the ultimate test for Battery D. During the last weeks of the war, the 129th positioned themselves for action for the final dand last time on the battlefields of Verdun. Final shots were fired just fifteen minutes prior to the Armistice taking effect. Battery D fired over 10,000 rounds during this war alone.

Battery D suffered no deaths during their combat missions, and the men felt lucky to be alive. They felt they owed their luck to "Captain Harry." They forged very close bonds that endured for the rest of their natural lives. All the men stayed in touch in some way. Even during his political career, Harry always fell back on his army buddies for support.

Harry's tour during WWI had a very recondite effect on his life. It had boosted his confidence. During war time, Harry had become close friends with some of the soldiers. But through it all, he carried a picture of Bess in his left breast pocket.

In 1919 following his discharge, Harry missed army life so much that he decided he wanted to rejoin the Federal Service again by joining the Officers' Reserve Corps. He even rose to the rank of colonel. He completed a final stint of actual active duty in 1933, and he was appointed commanding officer of the 379th Field Artillery. Harry attended unit training in the summers of 1936 - 1938. Harry was a strong advocate that the military should stay prepared as it was the best method of defense. He wanted to return to active duty when WWII broke out, but Staff General George C. Marshall declined him.

Today, Truman has a Veteran's Administration Hospital named after him located in Columbia, Missouri. During Truman's time in office as president, he helped with placing other needed Veterans Hospitals in other parts of the United States.

Chapter 3: Harry & Bess – And Political Beginnings

One month after returning from war, Harry and Bess got married on June 28, 1919, in a little Episcopal church in Independence, Missouri. If he had to be away from Bess on their anniversary, he always tried to send her a special letter. There are 1300 letters of courtship and letters after their marriage that still exist that Harry sent his Bess. For some reason, most of Bess's letters have not survived. They moved into the Gates-Wallace House at 219 North Delaware, where Bess had been living when her father killed himself. Harry let Bess's mother live with them because he knew that Bess felt responsible for her mother. She assured Harry it would only be a temporary situation, but Mrs. Wallace lived with them for 15 years!

A few months after Harry and Bess's wedding, Harry and one of his war buddies, Eddie Jacobson, opened what was then called a haberdashery. At first, business was great at their store, but it couldn't hold up during the acute economic recession of the 1920s. They had to close the clothing store in September 1922. Truman was almost bankrupt and very heavily in debt.

Bess and Harry wanted a child. Unfortunately, Bess had problems and two miscarriages. After four years, they had their first, and what was to be their only child, Mary Margaret, who was born February 17, 1924. They did not have a crib for baby Margaret, so they pulled a drawer from their dresser and used it as a baby bed. Little Margaret was frail and required a lot of medical attention, and this caused her to be doted on by Harry and Bess and all her extended family.

Harry loved little Margaret to the moon and back. He showered her with attention. When work kept him from home for some reason or other, he would be sure to include messages in his letters to his wife. One he wrote when Margaret was eight said, "Have you been practicing on your piano music? I'm going to want you to play all those exercises when I get home."

Harry, Bess, and Margaret were seen in public together a lot. They had even been dubbed "The Three Musketeers." Truman would sometimes joke that the three of them would probably make a good vaudeville act. Harry on the piano, Bess would manage, and Margaret would sing. Bess preferred to stay out of the limelight, but Harry was always ready to share with the most important people in his world.

Harry kept up with his friends from the National Guard. Many of them stopped by his shop when it was open. He joined several organizations, most of them civic in nature.

There were times that Harry had said he might like some day to try his hand at politics. In 1921 his chance came to him. A 'friend,' Jim Pendergast and his father, Mike, came to Harry and asked him if he would run for the County Court. Truman ran a close primary with five opponents. The regular election was a no-brainer. He won easily, beating his Republican opponent. Truman was now the Eastern Judge and served two terms as Presiding Judge. He had been chosen by the local political machine as it was at that time and he remained loyal to Mike and Tom. Harry was careful to sidestep the political corruption that seemed endemic to county politics. Harry worked hard all the time. He made sure that two county courthouses were constructed as promised and that the county's roads were improved.

One must know this background to know some of the behind the scenes scenarios that played into Harry's successes. At the turn of the century and well up into the 1940s, Kansas City politics were run mostly by Democrats of the Irish-Catholic Pendergast family. There was "Alderman Jim," – the saloonkeeper, and his baby brother Tom, who some called "Boss Tom." Jim was Harry's wartime buddy and the son of Mike, who was the younger brother of Boss Tom and Alderman Jim. Truman's political opponents made as much mud as they could of this connection to the Pendergasts. The issue, however, had no effect whatsoever on him winning elections to higher offices.

While serving as a County Judge, Harry appointed a board to develop a plan; then a survey was conducted of the county roads. Approval was sought for two separate bond votes to fund the road projects. Voters amazingly approved both bonds. The newly repaired roads would help the farmers get their products and livestock to market much easier and quicker.

Truman had it in his promise to build a new county courthouse in Kansas City, and to remodel the one in Independence. While researching other courthouses, Harry was impressed by the Art Deco style he found in the Caddo Parish Courthouse in Louisiana. Harry hired the architect as a consultant for the Kansas City courthouse. For the Independence, Missouri courthouse, Harry used the Independence Hall in Philadelphia as the model. Both projects were completed before Harry, Bess, and Margaret moved on to the United States Senate.

In 1924 Harry lost in the re-election due to a feud out in the county. Then in 1926, he was again elected to the county court as the presiding judge; and once again in 1930. During his years in this office, he oversaw the rebuilding of that counties roads, was involved in major construction projects, and successfully managed the finances of the county during the Great Depression's early years.

During 1930 and 1934, Harry sometimes would take refuge at the Pickwick Hotel in Kansas City. He had started having headaches and insomnia and had become increasingly tense, and the Pickwick was a place he could think and work uninterrupted. Truman started putting his thoughts down on hotel stationery. He talked in the papers about the county politics, personalities; he described corruption he had witnessed and some of the ethical dilemmas he had faced. His "Pickwick Papers" have come to provide remarkable insight as to the difficulties a future President struggles with before his career has really started.

In 1934, Truman wanted to run for Congress or Governor. He was very disappointed that Tom Pendergast had chosen others for these offices. Then out of the blue, Tom asked Harry to run for the Senate. Pendergast who was supporting Truman for his run and was known for his scrupulousness (Rumor had it that Pendergast made sure that the ballot boxes were stuffed). Harry ran as Pendergast had told him to and he won. So, December

31, 1934, Truman, the new Senator-elect and his wife and daughter thus arrived in Washington, D.C.

While Harry was a Congressman in 1938, as he drove through an intersection a car smashed into Harry's. The other driver said he did not see the stop sign. He said the stop sign was blocked by another parked car. Harry's car was totaled. Margaret recalls the entire accident. She felt they were lucky to have made it out alive.

In 1939, Pendergast was in deep trouble. He was very ill; his gambling was out of control, and he owed millions. He was indicted for tax evasion by the Grand Jury in 1939. He was convicted, then sent to prison for fifteen months as well as banned from politics for five years. The entire scandal was bad for Truman.

 In his 1940 re-election; it was much more difficult this time around. The Pendergast machine was now in total ruins. He had no campaign funds to draw on, and no support from President Roosevelt, so Harry "barnstormed" the state of Missouri, always emphasizing his experience in Washington. He later said it was the most bitter, mud-slinging campaign in the history of Missouri. Most people did not think he had a chance. He barely won by 8,000 votes. Harry, looking back later on his life, said that his years serving as a Senator were the happiest ten years of his life.

Harry said that the Senate was like a brotherhood, not like anything else and he was proud being a part of it. His prior work ethic and self-discipline had paid off. He was almost always in the office by 7:00 a.m., he worked on his tasks with due diligence and determination. Harry grew more confident in his abilities as a leader and a congressman.

When Senator Truman was beginning his second term in early 1941, America was getting ready for the war effort. As he started to respond to complaints of profiteering and overspending by the United States military expansion, he was sure that large arms contracts were being handed over on-the-basis of favoritism; not to the lowest bidder. It looked like the contracts were being given to the big companies at the expense of small firms that had no political influence. So, he started by visiting war plants and military installations across the country. He soon discovered gross mismanagement of defense dollars. This brought on a much larger investigation. Due to his findings that there were millions of dollars being wasted; the Senate acted quickly and organized a Special Committee to Investigate the National Defense Program, naming Truman as the chair.

This committee had been given broad powers to investigate the terms of the defense contracts, how they had been awarded, and how the contractors themselves performed. He wanted to know if they utilized small businesses and the effect of the defense program on labor. The committee, often at extreme odds with the military branches – became what was called a "sympathetic critic" and helped raise the public's confidence in how the war was being managed. There were estimates made of the amount of money that was saved by the Truman Committee that ranged as high as $15 billion. This work brought Truman into the spotlight for all of America to see.

Truman during his first term emerged as President Franklin D. Roosevelt's reliable ally during the "New Deal" programs. He worked to build strong bonds with all the labor unions.

In 1941, Truman began his second term just as the United States was preparing for war again. Truman convinced Senate leaders and the Presidential administration to let him lead a special Senate Committee, that was known as the Truman Committee. This committee was put in place to uncover and stop wasteful defense spending.

Harry had already warned the public of all the threats of Germany and Japan. He told them that the United States needed increased military preparedness.

Chapter 4: How Harry Became President

In July 1944, Harry was talked into running as vice-president with President Franklin D. Roosevelt. As a matter of fact, Roosevelt made a phone call asking if they had that contrary guy from Missouri lined up yet? Roosevelt told Harry if he wanted to break up the Democratic Party in the middle of war, that was going to be his fault! Then he supposedly slammed the phone down. Truman supposedly replied that he guessed he better say yes then. When Harry accepted the nomination for vice president, Bess was not happy about the fact whatsoever.

During the convention, noticed how bad Roosevelt looked, but no one was saying anything. It was doubtful even then that he would live out his term in office. It surely had to be on everyone's mind, and surely it was on Truman's.

Within 82 days after this oath, President Roosevelt died. President Roosevelt died in his sleep from a pulmonary embolism between 4:00 and 4:15 a.m., January 20, 1945, at his home on Sagamore Hill. Harry found himself being thrust into a role that he had never intended to play. But here he was, several hours after he was told of Roosevelt's death. Harry, still stunned, went to the White House to be given the oath of office, which Chief Justice Harlan Stone officiated. Harry later told the reporters, "I don't know if any of you fellas ever had a load of hay fall on you, but when they told me what happened yesterday, I felt like the moon, the stars and all the planets had fallen on me." Harry was now the thirty-third President of the United States. A job he had never wanted.

Truman later referred to his first year as President as a year of decisions. Everywhere he turned there were decisions. Big decisions that had to be made by him; Harry was to oversee the ending of the war in Europe. He helped lay important groundwork for the final stages of the war against Japan. Harry was the one who approved the two atomic bombs being dropped on Japan on August 6th against Hiroshima and on the 9th against Nagasaki of 1945. The bombs killed immediately; 100,000 people with as many as twice that number who died from the after-effects of radiation poisoning. Japan sued for peace August 10th of that same year. They surrendered September 2, 1945.

Even to this day, there are seemingly unanswered questions. Some declare that Harry needed to use the bomb vs. invade Japan. They felt if we invaded Japan it would cost us hundreds of thousands of lives of our American soldiers and felt that Harry made the only logical choice. For 20 years, this was the thought of many.

As World War II in Europe was ending, the German leader, Adolf Hitler, burrowed away in his refurbished air-raid shelter, took a cyanide pill, then shot himself with his own pistol while in Berlin. This was only two weeks into Truman's presidency, and shortly after the allies declared victory in Europe on May 7, 1945.

This same year also saw the formation of the United Nations and the increasing strain and confrontation with the Soviet Union. The origin of the United Nations was to bring order and to try to avoid future world wars.

Harry was also serving as president during the Nuremberg Trials. The Trials punished at least 22 Nazi leaders for the crimes they had committed; crimes against humanity. 19 of those 22 were found guilty.

Truman's entire presidency was 'ear marked' by important initiatives for foreign policy. Everything that Truman did in regards to foreign policy was to prevent the influence of the Soviet Union.

Not many presidents were as dedicated to their families as was Harry. His mother, Martha Ellen, lived into her nineties. Truman always called her "Mama." She passed away in 1947. She and Harry were very close. She was a die-hard Democrat and an astute observer of politics. Mama supported her son's career in politics avidly. In 1944, she was chairwoman of the first meeting of women workers in Harry's campaign for the vice presidency.

When Harry's mother would come to Washington to visit him, she would not sleep in Lincoln's bed since she was such a staunch Confederate sympathizer and still had hard feelings about the outcome of the Civil War.

Harry's brother John Vivian worked as the district director at the Federal Housing Administration. He kept Harry up to date on the political news in Missouri. Harry often consulted with Vivian before he made any decisions involving Missourians.

March 7, 1947, Harry has a diary entry that says, "the doctor tells me I have some cardiac asthma. Ain't that hell? It makes no difference; I will go on just as before. I have sworn the doctor to secrecy." The doctor in later years said he usually gave Harry fluid pills when he had problems with his heart.

In April of 1947, there was one person who died in New York City of smallpox. This prompted healthcare workers to give 6.35 million doses of smallpox vaccinations in 28 days. And of course, before visiting New York, Harry himself had been vaccinated with the smallpox vaccine.

In 1947 Harry had to campaign again to hold the office of the presidency. He stumped through the fall. He made many train tours across the country. These trips were called "whistle stop" speeches, and they were delivered from the back of the presidential train. The longest "whistle stop" trip lasted 15 days and covered 8,300 miles, and it took Harry from Pennsylvania all the way to California.

In 1948, the Jewish People developed the state of Israel in Palestine itself. The United States was one of the first to recognize it as a new nation. Harry, it was said, because of his Christian beliefs, felt strongly about the state of Israel.

January 12, 1948, a young lad of Sarasota, Florida, Rusty Gilliland, age 13 wrote to President Truman about a puppy that someone had recently given him. Rusty told him in the letter that he had heard that Harry might not keep the puppy and if he didn't that Rusty would be glad to give the dog a home and he would call him "Whitey."

The Cocker Spaniel pup, whose name was "Feller" had been a gift to Harry in December 1947. Harry gave the puppy to the family of Brig. Gen. Wallace Graham, Harry's personal physician.

The Truman's were just not into owning pets. Margaret had an Irish Setter, named "Mike." Margaret brought Mike to stay at the White House for a short time early in the Truman Presidency but soon gave him away to neighbors.

Election Day of 1948. Harry, Margaret, and Bess got up in Independence, Missouri that morning and voted in their hometown. When it got to be lunch time, Harry went to eat with several of his old friends. He then went alone to a local hotel and waited there for the returns. When the clock struck midnight, Harry was watching NBC, and the report stated that Dewey was expected to win, even though Harry had more than one million votes more than Dewey. Harry fell asleep. At four the next morning, Harry's secret service agents came in to wake him up. They told him he needed to turn on his radio. Harry was ahead now by two million votes and no doubt he was going to win! Wow, with this victory, Harry went home, got Margaret and Bess and they returned to Washington by way of St. Louis where reporters flashed the most famous photo of all of Truman's political career. It was of Truman holding a copy of the 'Chicago Tribune" newspaper that had the headline "Dewey Defeats Truman."

Dewey had 45.1 percent of the vote while Harry had 49.5 percent. Harry held 303 of the electoral college votes, and only 189 went to Dewey. Truman won because he gained the support of Roosevelt's coalitions "New Deal": Blacks, labor, farmers from the Midwest, Jews, and several of the southern states. Harry did not win the popular vote like he would have liked. But the electoral college won him his presidency.

Truman supported civil rights, and he pushed strongly for civil rights legislation for people of color. He was the first twentieth-century president to do so. In 1948, even over strong objections of conservatives in Congress, Army leadership, and top Defense Department officials, Harry ordered there would be no more separate units for black and white soldiers. He had integrated the US Armed Forces.

The most impressive display in Truman's honor was that of Presidential pomp and circumstance during his 1949 Inauguration. He had started out his presidency because of Roosevelt's death, but this time he had won on his own merits. Since the press had unanimously predicted that he would lose, this made it an even sweeter victory.   The first time Truman had been sworn in as president was very subdued following Roosevelt's death. This time was different, he had good reason to celebrate publicly, and he did. The war was over, and he had the freedom to celebrate in the grandest of style.

At the inauguration, Truman gave an unusually stirring speech. He watched the parade and even stayed way into the night at the Inaugural Ball, which at that time was to be held at the National Guard Armory at 10:00 p.m. and it seemed he enjoyed every second.

This inauguration introduced several "firsts":

• This was the first time the Inauguration was openly integrated; Bess and Harry made sure that minorities could attend every event and could stay in Washington Hotels.

• There was the debut of the Presidential Seal of the United States for the first time at an Inauguration.

• Harry was the first President-Elect to use two Bibles to be sworn in. He had one Bible opened to Matthew verse 5, no chapter was given; "And seeing the multitudes, he went up into a mountain: and when he was set, his disciples came unto him…. Exodus 20: "And God spoke all these words, saying, I am the Lord thy God, which have brought thee out of the land of Egypt, out of the house of bondage. Thou shalt have no other gods before me…."

• The 1949 Inauguration was the first ever to be televised, and it was estimated that 10 million Americans were glued to their televisions. More watched the event than any other event ever before.

The 1949 budget happened to be the most elaborate and expensive to that date. The Republicans that held seats in Congress were so sure that Dewey was going to win that they had allotted a huge budget of $80,000, which they actually went way over. For that day and time, it was the most ever spent for an inauguration.

- Grandstand for parade: $189,000

- Inaugural ball: $29,000

- Fireworks: $3,950

- Commemorative souvenirs: $7,600

The crowd was huge. More than 600,000 visitors were anticipated to be in Washington, D.C. for the inauguration. The parade itself was seven miles long. Trains were arriving in Washington, DC every two minutes. 5,000 were going to have to sleep in Pullman cars in the railroad yard.

From 1945 to 1948 he was Time Magazine's "Man of the Year."

Harry was the first U.S. President who would appear on live television and deliver an address from the White House. This took place on October 5, 1947. His 1949 Inauguration was also the first ever televised.

Harry was the only president during our modern era who did not have a college education, but it was not because he had not tried nor because he did not yearn for one.

In 1948, when Harry won the upset presidential re-election, Bob Hope sent him a personal one-word telegram: "Unpack." Harry was so amused by the telegram that he kept it with him in his desk that stood in the Oval Office.

In 1948, one of Harry's diary entries said, I go for my walk, and then I go to church. The preacher treats me like a church member and not like something from the circus. That is why I go.

Some feel it troubling that when they read Harry's memoirs that he saw the victory of Japan by use of the atomic bomb was because of the help of God.

From 1948 to 1952, Bess, Harry, and Margaret lived at the Blair House across the street from the White House while it was being renovated. The White House, the 140-year old mansion was in such bad shape and so structurally unsound from haphazard alterations here and there, that it was in serious need of repair. It would see the most radical renovation of the entire history of the White House. Truman would walk back and forth to work in his office through the West Wing. Harry was known on many occasions to call the White House "the big white prison." Harry hated air conditioning and always used fans in his office.

 On November 1, 1950, shortly after 2:00 p.m., what sounded like gunfire woke Truman from his afternoon nap in his bedroom upstairs. Within three minutes, there were 32 shots fired. It was two Puerto Rican nationalists. Griselio Torresola and Oscar Collazo had tried their best to shoot their way in to assassinate Harry. White House police and Secret Service stopped them. One attacker died after he had fatally wounded a White House policeman and injured two others. The other attacker was wounded, but he did survive, stood trial, and went to prison.

Harry Truman was "General." Bess Truman was "Sunnyside." These were the nicknames given to Bess and Harry by the Secret Service agents during his time in office.

Truman got along with the "paparazzi" of yesteryear and even got along with the reporters who covered the White House for the most part. He gave in to photographers and allowed them new status. They all called Harry the honorary president of "The One More Club," which came about by their constant cries for 'one more' photo of the president. Columnists and publishers were another mess altogether. In Harry Truman's view, most of them were probably Republicans, and they were providing hostile and extremely biased coverage of his presidency. He was furious at criticism he got from syndicated columnists. There were Westbrook Peglar and Drew Pearson for example. Truman started calling them "guttersnipes" and "character assassins," and that their newspapers were nothing but "lie outlets."

Harry felt that a president could not always be popular. But you always had to be sincere, even if you didn't mean it.

During 1950-53, the United States was involved in the Korean Conflict. North Korea had invaded South Korea. North Korea being communist, this was unacceptable. Truman had the United Nations agree for the U.S. to go in and get the North Koreans out of the South. MacArthur even though indirectly, had insulted Harry by making announcements about policy as to how he would be handling this war. It would have been the direct opposite of the principles of US Military Leaders, who said we're not making it. He also strongly implied that the conflict should be turned into a full out war against China and the Soviet Union. It had been realized that the Soviets were supplying weapons, aircrews and war planes to North Korea. There was a scheduled meeting between Harry and MacArthur in Korea. MacArthur made the order that his plane land first and kept Truman's plane circling until after MacArthur's plan had come to rest. Harry took that act as a direct insult to the office of the President, and most believe to this day that it firmed Harry's decision to relieve MacArthur of his post. Therefore, the United States did not gain what it went to achieve in the Korean conflict.

Harry created the CIA during his presidency. He created it for informational purposes only. He wanted the CIA to gather information only for the president so that Harry could make better-informed decisions. At the end of his presidency and beyond, Harry felt he may have created a monster. The CIA was far reaching and doing much darker duties than what they had been assigned.

Another important issue during Harry's presidency was the Red Scare. It was like the Cold War between the United States and the Soviet Union and it increased during the late 1940s and the early 1950s; there was growing hysteria over a conceived notion of a threat posed by Communists living in the U.S.

(Communists were called "Reds" because of their allegiance to the red flag.

Harry ran with a routine while in the White House. It was like clockwork every day. He got up at 5:00 every morning, got dressed and walked vigorously one or two miles (and this was at the Army's 120-steps-per-minute pace). He would go around the White House grounds and through the neighborhood – wearing his suit and his tie. After the assassination attempt in 1950, his Secret Service agents would change his routine and take him to different undisclosed destinations so he could take these daily walks. He would come back then, get a rubdown, drink a shot of bourbon and eat a light breakfast which consisted of one egg, one piece of toast, one slice of bacon and one glass of skimmed milk. He tried every day to eat lunch with his Bess and then take a short afternoon nap. Usually, at mid-day, Harry would take a few laps in the White House swimming pool. He always swam with his eyeglasses on. In the evenings, if he had no business meetings, Harry and Bess would enjoy cocktails, eat a quiet dinner, listen to some music or watch a movie. Once or twice during the week he would try and slip away to a poker party with his buddies at someone's private home, and he seldom returned before midnight. Harry loved to hear and to tell dirty jokes and loved visiting with his old army buddies. He would relax by taking trips on the presidential yacht, the Williamsburg, or by vacationing in Key West, Florida at the Naval base. Harry rarely took Bess and Margaret on these excursions, but always invited his army buddies.

In 1954 Harry suffered a gallbladder attack while watching a play. He was taken into emergency surgery, and it was successful. After the gallbladder surgery, Harry was given an antibiotic that he suffered a severe reaction from. Harry said he had 'hives inside of him and outside.' For a while, he could not keep food down. Within a few days, he recovered.

December 22, 1963 – Harry Truman had concerns about the CIA. He felt that it was time to take another look at the true purpose of the operations of the CIA. Harry stated that he developed the CIA to be the long arm of the president, to gain information that could help him as president make the right decisions. It would seem obvious that a President's role in his office is only as effective as the information he receives. The President must know what is going on all over the world.

Every president has at his disposal the information that has been gathered by all the intelligence agencies. That would be the Department of Defense, State, Interior, and Commerce and others who are constantly gathering extensive information.

It just seems that by the time the information was reaching the president, it was all conflicting. It felt like it was slanted as to the department that was giving the report.

For some time, Harry had been worried by how the CIA was diverting from its given assignment. It seemed it had become more operational and had started being a policy-making arm of the Government, not something it had been set up to do. Harry felt this had been leading to trouble and may have made worse the difficulties in several explosive areas of our government and around the world.

Harry said that when he set up the CIA that it would be diverted and injected to times of peace and not cloak and dagger operations. Harry felt the CIA was now so removed from what it had intended to be used for that now it was looked at as something mysterious and sinister with foreign intrigue.

Chapter 5: Harry's Life After His Presidency

Margaret like her father had expressed an interest in music at a very early age. She, however, wanted to become a singer and not a pianist. She attended George Washington University and majored in history. Then in 1947, even though her singing teacher advised against it and felt she needed more training, Margaret made her debut on the Ford Motor Company's "Sunday Evening Hour."

Margaret performed quite frequently in public. She was even on a what was considered a successful thirty-city tour in 1947, and she was said to show some promise. However, music critics were not nice about Margaret. And they did not offer good reviews of her performances.

Margaret finally gave up her music career when she fell in love and married Edward Clifton Daniel who was known to all as a successful assistant foreign newspaper editor in New York. Harry supposedly said in a letter to a friend of his, Dean Acheson, that he guessed he approved. "He seems to be a nice guy, and I guess if Margaret likes him I'll have to be satisfied." "As every old man who has a daughter, I feel that I am worried and I just hope that everything works out alright." They were married in 1956. Clifton Truman Daniel, Harry's first grandson, was born in 1957. Margaret gave birth to three more boys: William, Harrison, and Thomas.

Margaret was also known as a writer of murder mysteries, and they were popular. All of them were set, where else, but in Washington, D.C.

Truman, after he left the presidency, retired back to Independence in 1953. For almost two decades of his remaining life, he was happy just to be "Mr. Citizen," as he sometimes referred to himself. He spent his time writing, reading, taking walks, and lecturing. He even wrote a book with the title, "Mr. Citizen."

Harry traveled a little, even including a trip in 1953 when he drove to New York. During the journey, he was stopped by a policeman on the Pennsylvania Turnpike. He had been caught making an illegal change of lanes. That was the only attempt at driving a long-distance Harry made after he left the presidency.

He found great joy in his presidential library. When he was at the library, Harry loved receiving important guests. He met scholars that were studying his presidency, and he enjoyed speaking to groups of children from schools. His trademark feistiness was still there; he informed a young professor of history that he needed to go home and read his books some more and then come back and interview him again.

Now in history, there had been no laws allowing pensions for former Presidents. Harry and Bess lived solely on his pension from the military for his service in World War I. It was $112.56 a month. While in office as president, Harry had been making $100,000 a year.

Harry had made sure that Congressmen had benefit packages when they left office, but there was no such package for the President. But, after Harry left office, Congress did vote to give the president a benefits package on leaving the presidency of $25,000 a year.

His pet name for Bess was, "The Boss." But there was no doubt; he did not mind her being the boss; he loved her with all his heart.

After his presidency, Harry was bombarded with offers for speaking engagements or commercial products they wanted him to plug. Harry told all of them no. He was not stupid; they didn't want him, not Harry Truman, they wanted to have the endorsement of the President. He was not about to compromise the distinction of the office of the president.

For all the criticism, he took while in office; historians now believe that Harry Truman was among one of the United State's best Presidents.   The legacy of Truman has become more impressive and more clear in the years since he left office.

To write his memoirs, Harry had to take a loan out at the Missouri Bank. He sold his book rights for $670,000. By the time, he paid his ghostwriters and taxes took their two-thirds; Harry was left with $37,000.

In 1955, Harry finally published his first book of memoirs- "Decisions and Memoirs." His second book was released in 1956 – "Years of Trials and Hope." Harry had hired ghostwriters and various research assistants to help him, and thus, the books were disorganized, and they offered a sad account of the Truman presidency.

Harry stayed active in American politics even after leaving the White House. Eisenhower annoyed and made Harry angry. He regularly let the public know what he thought about his administration's policies and its' politics. The personal relationship between the two of them only got worse through the eight years of Eisenhower's presidency.

Harry dealt better with Kennedy and Johnson. He had some reservations about Kennedy at first; he thought he was probably too young and maybe too Catholic to be much of a success as a Democrat. Once in Office, however, Kennedy and Jackie charmed Harry. He got along fine with Johnson, whom he enjoyed being around, but he could never stand Nixon.

In 1956, Bess and Harry took a trip to Europe, and they were a smashing hit. Britain awarded him with an honorary degree in Civic Law from Oxford University. This was an event that moved him to tears. He and Bess spent the day with his friend Winston Churchill at the Chartwell Estate for what would be the last time he would see his friend. They had lunch with the Queen at Buckingham Palace. This was a first for Bess who had never been to Europe. While in Europe they saw Venice, Florence, Pompeii, Brussels, Salzburg, and Amsterdam - seeing all the historical places Harry had read about since he was a kid.

 On returning to the United States, he gave support to Adlai Stevenson's second bid for President. Initially, he had favored

Democratic Governor Averell Harriman of New York but changed his mind.

In 1964, a bad fall in his bathroom of his home caused severe limitation in his physical abilities. It was enough, that he was not able to keep up his daily presence at his presidential library that he loved so much.

In 1965, President Lyndon B. Johnson signed what we know as the Medicare bill at the Truman Library. After the signing, he gave the first two Medicare cards to Bess and Harry Truman. Truman had fought non-stop for government health care during his entire time as President. He saw his dream come to fruition.

Harry has been pictured on the 8 cent US commemorative postage stamp released on May 8, 1973, which was the anniversary of his birth, right after his death. He was pictured on the 20 cent US definitive postage stamp series, the Great Americans that was issued January 26, 1984. He was also pictured on the 4-cent commemorative postage label issued by the Independent Postal System of America in 1973. (The Independent Postal System of America, of course, is now defunct.)

When Truman turned 80, he was asked to address the United States Senate as part of a new rule that would allow former presidents to be granted "privilege of the floor." Harry was so overcome with emotion by the honor and the reception that he could hardly deliver his speech.

Chapter 6: Harry & Bess – A Time to Mourn

President Truman's Obituary

(From page 1 of the New York Times, December 27, 1972)

TRUMAN, 33RD PRESIDENT IS DEAD; SERVED IN TIME OF FIRST A-BOMB,

MARSHALL PLAN, NATO, AND KOREA

Funeral to be Tomorrow in Independence Library

By B. Drummond Ayers Jr.

Special To The New York Times

KANSAS CITY, Mo., Dec 26 – Harry S. Truman, the 33d President of the United States, died this morning. He was 88 years old.

Mr. Truman, an outspoken and decisive Missouri Democrat who served in the White House from 1945 to 1953, succumbed at 7:50 a.m., central standard time, in Kansas City's Research Hospital and Medical Center. He had been a patient there for the last 22 days, struggling against lung congestion, heart irregularity, kidney failure and inflictions of old age.

In the more than seven years he was President, from the time of Franklin Delano Roosevelt's death; it suddenly elevated him from the Vice Presidency until he himself was succeeded by Dwight David Eisenhower, Mr. Truman left a major mark as a world leader.

He brought mankind face to face with the age of Holocaust by ordering atomic bombs dropped on Japan, sent American troops into Korea to halt Communist aggression in Asia, helped contain Communism in Europe by forming the North Atlantic

Treaty Organization and speeded the postwar recovery of
Europe through the Marshall Plan.

His domestic record was somewhat less dramatic, for his
proposals were often premature. He ended up on the losing
sides of fights other Presidents later won – Federal healthcare,
equal rights legislation, low-income housing.

His other legacies were perhaps less tangible but no less
remembered – the morning walk, the "Give 'em hell" campaign
that nipped Thomas E. Dewey at the wire, the desk plaque that
proclaimed "The Buck Stops Here!" and the word to the timid
and indecisive "If you can't stand the heat, get out of the
kitchen."

Towards the end of his struggle for life, the former President
weakened steadily. Early yesterday his doctors warned that
death might come "within hours."

When it came, the doctors announced that the cause was "a
complexity of organic failures causing a collapse of the
cardiovascular system."

A state funeral will be held Thursday in nearby Independence,
Mr. Truman's hometown, to mark his passing. Much of the
ceremony will be subdued and private at the family's request.

State funerals are conducted only for former commanders in
chief, although the President can direct that a state funeral be
held for an individual. Modifications in state funerals, which
usually cover 4 or 5 days with considerable ceremony, are made
at the request of the family, as in this case.

President Nixon has declared the day of burial, Thursday, to be a
day of national mourning. The American flag is to be flown at
half-mast for thirty days.

The former President's body will lie in state at the Truman
Library in Independence from 1:35 p.m. tomorrow until 11:00
a.m. Thursday. Burial will follow on the Library grounds at a
spot chosen by Mr. Truman himself.

President Nixon will fly to Kansas City tomorrow afternoon, then go to the library to lie a wreath at the base of Mr. Truman's coffin. Although it is understood that the President's name was included on the official list of persons invited to attend the funeral, it was expected that, in keeping with the subdued and private nature of the ceremony, he would not stay overnight for the funeral service and burial.

Tomorrow morning the coffin will be transported to the Library on a route that will pass the Victorian Truman home on the way from the Carson Funeral Home a few blocks away.

The service, scheduled to begin at 2:00 p.m. Thursday, will be held in the Library's 250-seat auditorium. Attendance will be by invitation. Burial will follow immediately.

Mrs. Truman At Home

The Truman family has asked, that in lieu of flowers, friends make donations to the Library or charities. At the time of his death, Mr. Truman's wife, Bess, 87, was at their home in Independence, having spent most of the day with her husband and his friend, Dr. Wallace Graham.

Mr. Truman's only child, Mrs. Clifton Daniel of New York also was at the home. She flew to Kansas City last night for a brief visit with her father.

Today, Mr. Daniel, an associate editor of the New York Times, was met at the Kansas City airport by his wife and Mrs. Truman. The four Daniel boys, Thomas Washington, 4; Harrison Gates, 7; William Wallace, 11; and Clifton Truman, 13 – are to arrive tomorrow.

The only other immediate Truman survivor is the former President's 83-year-old sister, Miss Mary Jane Truman, of Grandview. She has been a patient of Research Hospital since suffering a fall several weeks ago, and was notified of her brother's death in a nearby room within minutes.

The hospital announcement of Mr. Truman's death was released at 8:10 a.m. by Wayne E. Conery, an assistant administrator. It was the 80th bulletin concerning the former President's illness and stated:

"The Hon. Harry S. Truman, the 33d President of the United States, died at 7:50 a.m. at Research Hospital and Medical Center. The cause of death has not been determined. Dr. Wallace Graham was present. Mrs. Truman and Mrs. Clifton Daniel were notified at 7:52 a.m. Funeral arrangements have not been finalized. It is the wish of the family that friends make donations to the Harry S. Truman Library Institute, Independence, Mo or the charities of their choice."

Mr. Truman's final illness was the eighth to put him in Research Hospital. The others had been four different cases of infections of the intestines, a hernia, appendicitis, and a broken rib.

The final period began during late November with a minor case of his lungs being congested. Initially, the doctors just treated him at home.

By December 5th, the doctors ordered he be hospitalized. The congestion was much worse, his heart which was already weak from a long struggle of hardening of the arteries started beating irregularly under all the strain.

When he was first admitted to the hospital, his condition was considered as "fair." By the next night, it had changed to "critically ill" when his blood pressure started dropping, and it became 80/60, and his pulse went to 120. His temperature was 102.8, and then his breathing became labored.

Harry fought back and was moved to "serious" condition by the end of his first week, and he told the doctors he felt better.

Then, a few days later, just when his lung and heart seemed to be stabilizing, his kidneys began to fail. His condition was changed to "very serious" as his blood urea nitrogen began to elevate.

Harry again fought back; he told the doctors at the end of the second week that he "felt all right," even though they had decided not to use the dialysis machine due to his hardened arteries. Mrs. Daniel returned to New York.

The doctors began feeding him a solution that was to reduce impurities from his blood. There were immediate results and reduction. But this did not last long. Truman's blood pressure dropped, his temperature rose again, and his condition went back to "critical." Doctors and nurses started monitoring him constantly. His breathing had again become labored, his kidney output had decreased, fluid was building up in his lungs, and his heart was beginning to flutter.

On Christmas morning, Harry was so weak that the family was told that death could come any time, but "within hours."

Harry died on the sixth floor of the hospital, a 500-bed facility that he helped dedicate in 1963. There were two green and red Christmas bells hanging in the window. The window looked east toward the completed football and baseball stadiums of the Harry S Truman Sports complex.

The cost of his private room at that time was $59.50 a day. In Harry's case, it was paid by private medical insurance and Medicare. Harry held Medicare card number 1. Even though he had not been able to push this plan through while he was president, Lyndon Johnson was successful and came to Independence in 1965 to sign the Medicare Act in the Truman Library. It was a final political victory for Harry S. Truman.

In his last will and testament, that he executed January 1959, he carefully divided his estate, valued at $600,000 to his daughter and wife. He left to the Masonic Lodge a plot of land located in Grandview, Missouri. To his nieces, nephews and their children, he left $15,000 to be divided.

Harry had told Bess he did not want to lie in state in Washington D.C. He did approve the plans that were made for his funeral, however. He attended several of the planning sessions, and told them he was going to regret missing such a "fine show." The funeral, when the time came, was simplified even more from the original plan, and was more of what the family had in mind.

Bess vetoed plans for anything elaborate for the funeral. She arranged an Episcopalian service in Harry's beloved Truman Library in the auditorium. She had the Grand Masonic Leader of Missouri and a Baptist Minister conduct the proceedings. Truman was buried out in the courtyard of his library, where a simple stone epitaph was etched with his own words. It gave his date of birth, his date of death, his date of marriage to Bess. The dates he served and names of every public office he held.

BESS TRUMAN RITES HELD IN MISSOURI

By NATHANIEL SHEPP

Published: October 22, 1982

Independence, Mo., Oct. 21 – Bess Truman was laid to rest today on a grassy hillside alongside her husband, Harry S Truman, after a simple ceremony in this quiet city where they met and to which they returned after Truman stepped down as President in 1953.

The private funeral at Trinity Episcopal Church was attended by 145 invited guests and dignitaries, including Nancy Reagan, Rosalynn Carter and Betty Ford. It was brief and simple, in keeping with the image of quiet dignity that was the hallmark of the former First Lady.

It was not customary for Episcopalians to have eulogies and none were given today for Mrs. Truman, who died Monday at the age of 97. "All here today are Mrs. Truman's eulogy," said the Rev. Robert L. Hart, who presided at the service in the red brick church where she was confirmed in 1903 and where she and Harry were married in 1919.

"Your presence as family and friends is a 'well-spoken word' in testimony to a life well-lived," he said. "Bess Truman was a Christian woman, a woman of integrity, graciousness, and intelligence."

The ceremony began at 11:00 a.m. when the shiny redwood coffin was carried into the church by pallbearers, followed by

Mrs. Truman's daughter, Margaret, her husband, Clifton Daniel, and their four sons. The invited guests filed in afterward.

Two of Bess's grandsons, Clifton and William, read scriptures during the service. "The Spirit of the Lord God is upon me; because the Lord hath anointed me to preach good tidings unto the meek," 23-year-old William read from the book of Isaiah, "He hath sent me to bind up the broken-hearted, to proclaim liberty to the captives and the opening of the prison to them that are bound."

The street in front of the church was cordoned off by the police to keep onlookers away. After the 20-minute service was completed, a 40-vehicle procession slowly made its way to the burial site in the courtyard of the Harry S Truman Library, about a mile away.

Mrs. Truman's coffin, draped with deep green fabric was placed on a bier next to the Vermont granite marker over her husband's grave. A large bouquet of yellow roses, her favorite flower, were placed on top of the coffin and a bouquet of red roses were placed beside it. To the rear, more flowers surrounded the gilded cover that was to be placed over her grave.

After the guests had entered the courtyard, passing along either side of a row of red and white flowers, Mr. Hart recited the Committal, sprinkling earth on the coffin in the pattern of a cross when he reached the segment "ashes to ashes, dust to dust."

"The Lord bless her and keep her; the Lord make her face to shine upon Him and be gracious unto her, the Lord lift up his countenance upon her and give her peace," he said.

After the ceremony, which lasted 12 minutes, the dignitaries attended a private reception in a wing of the library. Mrs. Reagan left shortly after the reception began, reportedly because she had a full schedule.

Several guests attended a news conference after the funeral and praised Mrs. Truman. "We can feel only a sense of gratitude to have had a lady like Bess Truman as a First Lady, friend, and neighbor and we wish her family the best," said Governor Christopher Bond.

When Bess died ten years after Harry, her marker read, "First Lady of the United States."

September 6, 2000: Grandson of former President Truman dies from being hit by a cab on Park Avenue over the weekend. The accident investigation is still ongoing.

The victim, William Wallace Daniel, 41, was the son of Margaret Truman-Daniel and Clayton Daniel, who was known as the former managing editor of the New York Times.

Mr. Daniel's colleagues and friends recalled his great humor. His girlfriend, Mimi Graber said that Daniel was always ready to do something on the spur of the moment, like hang gliding across the Grand Canyon.

January 29, 2008 - Margaret Truman Daniel, radio and television host, has died today in Chicago. She was 83. Her son Clifton Truman Daniel announced her death. She died after a brief illness.

Margaret adored her father. She wrote a biography in 1973 of her father "Harry S Truman" (William Morrow), that went on to become a Book-of-the-Month Club selection.

Margaret said she had never thought of writing about history, but being a child of a president; in such a world of power, and in such a cataclysmic time, one would be expected to write something about this man that belonged to the people and history, and to help others to get to know him as only a daughter would.

Conclusion

Thanks again for taking the time to read this book!

You should now have a good understanding of the life and journey of Harry S. Truman.

I hope that you found this book to be both informative and enjoyable.

If you enjoyed this book, please take the time to leave me a review on Amazon. I appreciate your honest feedback, and it really helps me to continue producing high quality books.